Day Mattar is a cheeky queer poet
They are the co-founder of Queer Bodies poetry collective, and facilitate poetry workshops with various art organisations in the UK. Their poetry pamphlet, *Springing from the Pews*, was published with Broken Sleep Books. Day's poems come from the body, they use poetry as a tool to explore links between the psychological and the physical, the somatic and the sensual. Can a poem make you jump? Is your heart beating faster?

Brendan Curtis is a Liverpool based drag artist, writer, performer and chef. He produces and hosts EAT ME, a local 3 course drag dinner cabaret, Preach! a queer disco and SPEW a scratch night for new queer work. He home birthed Queer Bodies in between lockdowns with Day Mattar and the help of many others.

QUEER BODIES is a poetry collective based in the North of England, whose goal is to nourish, cultivate and connect queer identifying writers. They host and facilitate poetry workshops, performances, courses, and residencies, with a focus on queering the literary canon and producing new queer work. Their latest project QUEER ICONS was supported by Arts Council England, One September, Homotopia, DADA Fest, Writing on the Wall, Heart of Glass, Broken Sleep, First Take, and Creative Futures.

QUEER BODIES
Queer Icons Anthology

Edited by Day Mattar & Brendan Curtis

—

ISBN: 978-1-915079-28-2

—

brokensleepbooks.com

—

—

Cover designed by Aaron Kent

—

Typeset by Aaron Kent

—

Edited by Day Mattar & Brendan Curtis

Broken Sleep Books
Rhydwen
Talgarreg
Ceredigion
SA44 4HB

Broken Sleep Books
Fair View
St Georges Road
Cornwall
PL26 7YH

Contents

Queer Bodies

Queer Icons

Introduction

what the poet (a mother) might say
for the Queer Bodies

unbutton the silk blouse
      of your shame & lift it to
            this bonfire of language

admire the flirt of a flame
      how silk coils & blushes as
            shame unravels for language

scan the beach for a shell
      and name it after a loss
            a gift for the pyre to ponder

study how stubbornly grief
      can glow and splinter
            in the heat of language

gather sea holly on high dunes
      so I might watch you sweat
            in search of a spined beauty

so you might not notice as
      I climb this furnace for a poem
            in hope that you might write it

— *Day Mattar*

I was not given a road map, a time line or cue cards.

I can't remember seeing any one openly bisexual in the media for the first 20 years of my life.

I sought out images, destroyed the family computer, trawled song lyrics, created avatars in chat rooms and read anything remotely queer adjacent – thirsty for a diagnosis or a definition: what was I?

When our lives and feelings are invalidated by polite society, our bodies ascribed 'non-normative' status or our existences de-legitimized by our parents or the powers that be - it becomes a necessary act of survival to dignify one's experience and to seek out selves relatable to one's own.

Maybe this is why we are so engrossed in the processes and languaging of identification – as a response to our erasure and absence from the public realm. In living our lives as 'Other'– we pose a threat to the factory setting and those that benefit from its productions. Maybe this is why we are often so insistent, stubborn and LOUD - Why we push boundaries and take up SPACE with our vivacity, erudition and ebullience - courting visibility with alter egos, sequins, waistcoats and rainbows – because it has rarely been given to us freely.

Queer people venerate and mythologize our ancestry, icons and elders because so little of them was recorded - or because they are dead.

We are pressed to inscribe ourselves within a history that denies our influence - and when even our god rejects us, we project ourselves onto the heavens and create our own cosmology of divas, deities and drag things. We search restlessly for shreds, evidence and secret histories – and then, tentatively, we push the fractured pieces together - safety pin, tattoo, collage and appliqué it all into a semi-coherent sense of self.

Isn't this alone an act of supreme innovation, creativity and alchemy: to build one's own self from nothing?

Culturally, of course, we are pioneers of iconography - creating waves, starting movements and paradigm shifts in music, design, art and computing. You'll often find us communicating through another/s tongue - gay men's speech is 'queer coded' through divas in old hollywood, our culture's are appropriated by the state and our words and images 'sampled' by straight artists - simultaneously diluted and distilled - but... like a peacock's plume, an exotic dance or the flick of a wrist - the message is transmitted. The queers speak in hankerchief code, innuendo, craigslist posts and plaid - we created our own vernaculars, lore and sacred texts – because our lives depended upon it - so, we could say, without words: you are safe here. I am like you.

In many ways, our difference, our Otherness and resistance to assimilation are among the few things that define and unite us as a 'queer community':

In Jay Farley's poem inspired by Andre Bagoo inspired by Thom Gunn – we hear echoing voices, an alternative lineage and commonality being traced. In many of these works you may experience a polyphony – at times individuating, and, at others, morphing into singularity.

It is a precious type of prayer that happens when groups of queer people come together. This collection is a transmission of holiness, beauty and truth– I entreat you to listen to our song - perhaps you will hear your own voice in the chorus

— brendan curtis / auntie climax - to mandy romero

Katie Jukes

Ode to my Beloved's Back

your back
my drum
snare drum
drum tongue
flesh thumb
bone numb
skin drum
tongue drum
your back
my beat
beat bone
bone street
bare feet
stone steep
drum beat
lie back
flesh heat
soft beat
birth seat
bowl shell
heart swell
long bell
soft shell
your back
bone rack
my drum
steep stack
snare drum
drum tongue
flesh thumb
bone numb
skin drum
tongue drum

Monogamy

after Jericho Brown

I will not leave you
standing in the kitchen

the Wronged Wife of number twenty-two
I will not break the promise

made on that Scottish beach,
sunlight rupturing rain

in silver ribbons.
I promise you:

I will not slam my ears shut
I will not leave you lonely

crying over yellow daffodils
nor abandon you

the way a jealous woman spits
back the taste of death

like a knuckle caught in her throat
no I will not kiss another woman

just for the thrill and if I do
I promise you I will

be thinking of the tango
we chose those nights.

When I leave it will not be
because our boy screamed

your name, nor because you
asked for water

and I brought fire.
When I leave I will do it

the way we always said:
your legs wrapped

around my stomach, both of us
gripping the bars

Self-Portrait As A Sand-Pit

Mothers in the pirate park are sizzling
children play at sharks as the tide drives in
& catches them open-mouthed gossiping
about husbands & sex after the o so
unsexy birth of their children how they
can't get it out of their minds

                       how Mothers
must keep smooth and clean as a blue
flag beach and the Mothers shave their
legs armpits bikini lines wear make-up for
the school run & the tide

                     is driving further in &
children run from swing to sand-pit as the
foam of salt water catches their bare heels
and they begin digging holes hills roads o
this mother is dressed in timber she wants
to be left to settle to be an oak home

wild poppies brambles wind swirling
patterns across her face rain pock pocking
o she loves her children but not like this
a rumbling at the bottom of the sand-pit

Eva Lewis

Daughter, Hardly, There

The daughter has begun to write about herself in the third person.
This makes it easier for her to write about herself as a daughter.
It also makes it harder to picture herself as having a body.

The daughter paces the beach. The pacing **is** a figure
of eight. The beach is a figure of eight. The daughter picks up
a shell, hears her blood vessels wave at her.

One daughter is a polar bear, one an arctic
fox. At night I hear her scratching the bins like mosquito bites.
Attached to one ear is a limpet of sound. Her father,

the shell satiating an echo. A recording of his hands
is made to accompany an audio reconstruction
of the sea in a meditation app. Instructed to close

their eyes, clients picture the world the metal
inside their phones has detonated.

Daughter, There, Hardly

[17:09]

A portable dereliction in the storm.

Watching my mother's hands
make me dinner again as I salt
the potatoes bring the oven
to fever. I want to downsize

but no one is selling. The boxes
in my mouth become too heavy
to lift above my tongue.
I keep ice in silhouettes.

In my body I keep the ice my mother
says with cinched love, in old beach

buckets. I want to be held. So I
hold my breath trying to trap

a girl in that open-shut.

[17:11]

Hole makes its repetitions in breath,
breath repeats slow zero.

The daughter uses the same coordinates to say her name
as she uses for her hunger.

[21:22]

Inside the chimney
is every tool of a birds

-nest we call pyre. Struck into smoke to keep the body
warm. We thread rooms into ourselves. Soon I am

constructing my hallways. Soon I am drowning in who
I used to be. Wandering in a body full
of acknowledgments.

[22:17]

From here the scream is in the past.

The past is the light stain
of sun thinning to horizon.

You stare so long it stays
as the blind spot where the hill

zips the setting into night.

[23:51]

Listing each friction of a sharp object
with a scar. Making a geography
of the body. Mountains that contain
me as their ingredients. The line of
a house, receding to thin lips in the distance.

[8:13]

At some point, morning.
What the sun has puked up on the carpet,
a window-slab of bile.
The daughter associates this particular keyhole with a wound.

[10:36]

A throat with excess vodka
as a green exit sign.
A year or more inside a homeless glamour.
All summer wings evict us from our house, flying ant's braille the
kitchen in monosyllabic black caution
In the past I looked at this house and said yes.
Today the daughter is morning-laden.
Pills come with a magic carpet.

[15:07]

The mirror, one magpie.
In one socket, an eye, in one socket, a plug.
I have folds where I want to be folded, the exact creases of a swan
under specific conditions, the right hands.

[15:09]

It's a habitat to live inside memory.
My habit is memory so I miss you
where you centre me, soft hands
curled like wings during cocoon.

[15:12]

To call love home is to insinuate a leaving, something
a daughter could outgrow.

/Let me call you, instead, a body.
/Let me call you, instead, memory

my muscles arc into, like soft foam remembering
the shape of a dream.

[16:29]

This moment becoming the daughter's body, your tattoos
wording her arms.

Today I am symptomatic of large rock
arrowing towards sky. Mountain,

an elasticated prayer. The daughters lapse in
sertraline comes with the temporary

frostbite of her ghost.

There, Hardly Daughter

0.   Tidying light into the edges & corners of mountains,

1.   Looking at the recall of daughter in the lake.

1.   Sun a red fence she cannot get to.

1.   The air stings like a rash of pollen, but wind is careful, a pillow

1.   Smothering her face without ventilation.

1.   She walks through the gate of Kate Bush and becomes dance.

1.   Leaves her chance to rust with the gold afternoon grass.

1.   At the edge of her fiction was a trim of Adrianne, with gaps

1.   Close to blue between her teeth.

1.   The sun configured the exact structure of a lie.

1.   She found the clouds to be paraphrasing her sexes, her endeavours.

1.   A clique of mountains.

0.   An assortment of moons.

Jay Mitra

If Lazarus did not want to live

would you still call him Miracle?
his soul pulled back into decaying skin
and soft linen. did none of you think to ask

do you even want to come back?

his bandages fall like curtains
guillotines the end of Act Three.
he staggers onto the world's stage
and performs a loving tragedy.

this is what you do for family.

they throw thorned roses.
grin. Lazarus knows ingratitude is a sin.
and so, each catch is a cutting encore,
a reluctant second half.

Lazarus is a rewritten epitaph.

they say whoever believes in love, receives life
that even physical death can never take away.
when my deadname leaves my mother's mouth
Jemima is resurrected in my parents' house.

my binder becomes burial cloth

unravels onto the living room carpet.
as my mother hugs me, her feet trample fabric.
my life—a play written by her womb,
my protest is a scene that didn't make the cut.

and still, i hug my mother back.

Objectophilia

I used to judge people for it,
widen my eyes at the guy
in Ripley's Believe It or Not
who married his car.
figured he was insane,
delusional,
lonely.

Now look at me—
cowering under the covers,
sheltering from the cold.
My bed a grimy bunker
in an uncaring world.
On unwashed sheets, my feet
seduced by a whirr of heat.

There is something erotic
in the way electrons move
through the air's hot breath—
the duvet, too, becomes erect.
My dazed eyes droop
gooseflesh thawed by ecstasy
a blissful buzz spreads

through my forlorn body.
This steady hum
a loving lullaby.
This warmth is holy,
heavenly, ejaculatory.
Its plastic body and I,
engaged in surreal intimacy.

For some, it's a hairdryer
held under the covers.
For me, it's a space-heater.
Objectophilia:
the love of something
that never asks for anything.
Not an 'I love you' or a 'thank you.'

When you feel lonely
do you make the air hug you too?

Springtime

I unfurl
under tenderness.
the warmth of a voice
a soft crescendo of heat
like dawn delicately evaporating
dewdrops. Palms push,
and diaphanous petals spread apart.
before, I was a closed white rose,
a bud yet to breathe
but you
you sound like springtime.
and I
unfurl unafraid.

Jo Mary Watson

Concert Band 2019

Alternative title: bottled up

Bulbous glass bottle
lying on its side
the ship is the shape
of your bass guitar.

cork vibrating
with every single sound
your fingers make
on the strings – ropes

you knot together
ideas forming a truth
I already knew
knots that untie me

the cork pops out silently
no fireworks
for something that's a beginning
but nothing new.

your baseline controls the tides
waves breaking over dry land
in the rhythm of my heart
beating on my sleeve.

your siren song
causes shipwrecks for men
but I am baptized
by the water surrounding you.

Message sent from a ship called Hope *received by a lighthouse looking over a stormy sea:*

-.-- --- ..- / .-- ..-.. / - ..... / ..-. ... .-. ... - / -- .- -.- .. -. --. / -- ./ ..-.
. . .-.. / .... .- ..-. . .-.-.- / -.-- --- ..- / .-- ..-.. / - ..... / ..-. ... .-. ... - /
.-- ..-.. -.-. --- -- -- ..-. --. / -- ./ - --- / -.-. .- .-. .-. .-.-- / -- -.-- / ....
. .- .-. - / --- -. / -- -.-- / - --- -. --. ..- ./ .-.. --- ..- -.. / .- -. .-.. / .-.
.-. --- ..- -. ..-.-.- / .. / .-- .- .-. / ... --- / .-.. --- ... - / -.... ..-. --- .-.. /
-.-- --- ..- / ..-. --- ..- -. -.. / -- . .-.-.- / -.-- --- ..- / - .- ..- -- .-. .. - /
-- ./ .... --- .-. / - --- / -.... / ..-. .- . .-. .-.-.-

I made eyeballs

I opened a book
and found a language that I put
between your lips.

I painted by numbers
1 - 10: toes
1 - 10: fingers.

I spun a web
of veins through your body
delicate maze of life.

I remembered the ocean
in somebody else's eyes
and asked her if she could flood yours, too.

I framed a picture
of him and me, imagining the merge of our faces
into existence.

I played my violin
stringing notes together
that curved into your spine.

I forged a sword
only you can pull from the stone,
wrapped it in crimson velvet
and placed it in your chest
for you to lead with.

I wrote a poem.
It is you.

Frankie Blaus

YOU HAVE YOUR FATHER'S COCK

after Poem No. 2 by Yi Sang

This is how it works:

      addressed to the street I   wait
                          He/You   from the
             door   (signal)   recedes
     from the door   to
         the room
       to the skin
    the bed
cock
decent
kept to self
    how
is boring   I

don't know who you are   there is no way for you to tell
                 me   + so enters the eternal Argo(
                       whether   by   nauting
                            this ~~man~~ I   am
                            nauting his father/
                            in   being   nauted
                            by this ~~man~~ I remain
                            nauted by his father

                     his   father   has   certainly
         nauted   me)

Cold save the boys made in its bed   what's the difference
what's the difference what's the Difference What's the
difference What's the Difference What's the what what's the

What's the?   Difference.   After
all all there   is   is   is
after   is

David   David   David

confession   father   yr stone
yr heart   son   is not you
text of the   father   standing
sermon   son   burial
sowing   father   i see thru
your local   son   my touch
rapture   father   an echo
deeper   son   pushing
wider   father   itself against
up into   son   the particles
yr crown   father   o' the shell
+ the   son   my tap
bafflement   father   release of
of kings;   son   you i feel
feeling   father   its resistance
feelded   son   in this way
skyward   father   i am myself
the crown   son   touched
it cannot hold   holy   in turn
                             ghost

HOW DEEP MUST WE GO FOR US BOTH TO
FEEL
                                            THIS

+ then there   *The* David.

Is this how I was made = is this how mother/father did it
= (a specific time/place/perhaps) the room/prayer pushed
into body meaning ((I (meant to mean) once) practiced from
the first

cry the room   full of us is full of room we are
                            only ever praying to each Other ((I
                            (meaning) praying to our fathers
                            who put us here tucked away in
                            The) doing done

After all. What's the?   a moment Structured into
                            duvet for stay-siss(y)ing in
            Little   shriveled as a wish
                                            My furtive fucking

                            chrysalrisk
                            held/holding/hold/nestle/nestled/
                            in/feline/all fine these industrious
                            bedrooms Do they remember my
            My

                    name?

All there is   *is*

to imagine
to speak in terms of photography

it helps

example
when coated in the appropriate
solution

your negatives

will develop into

something like
expectation
an invert silhouette

the central figure

& there are none but me
philosophy of our relation
my sweet

making
my Godot
sweet symptom

you are nobody's fault really
what else could nobody expect

+   really

after all
a poem is
with the world behind it

you are all
white space

space; he made in me so he might fill it; as I (i) – as I
red against our black beneath; he; you; we; see; knowledge ceding;
something; leaves; a moan branching my apple; wet with me; thuds
-tain fruit; the ripe red comma of my throat; pushed up; pushed out
-membering himself into me; TONIGHT; solved for Now; the uncer
-ning like he was always there⁺ I (i); i (I); I (i); i (I) always there; re
the world my surface emer ges; to meet +; he is happe
in the world than i (I) wa s; this too is a leap; he is
see; the surface area of Sense; blooming; more
thing so all⁺nothing as goosepimple; he; you
displaced foundation presenting in some
-ding; +; he entered me; I (i) leap in after
-enning through; th e concrete surroun-
ahead of itself; ha ppenning to; happ
-ressed into my life like life happening
we; the scene; anot her impossibility; p
-made rains I () will do my dance for
-nside; beneath; pro mise of the man
walked elliptical on desires line; deep; i
-ed⁺named; named f or; water; evidence
brings the weather in with him; a place name
daylike; not yet; where w e go next; tonight; he
-scrunched from horizon mongrel snout rising into
-stere streets; lit by unfinishe d moon; too-soon; a sun un
regurgitates a world; premature with us; undigestible to these au

THE EAGLE

first happened; tonight; he will split me colourful; tonight;
sharing my 19 like underage anything; this man the moment i (I)
tonight; my root; history⁺the silence from which it grew; him⁺me;

( ), OR; ALL THAT WALKING JUST TO
REACH EACH OTHER'S SKIN

Dylan James

your room, everyday, all the time

there's wolves out there - she said - but the moon's more beautiful
through a window - she said - let's stay in - she said - read theories
describing the rotations of planets - she said - she said - ours is the
heart that all objects orbit - she said - I'll paint us safe in saltwater
canvas - safe in four walls, four borders - she said - why stand up -
she said - we'll only lay down again - she said - but falling in tug of
war is part of the game - I said - and only kids cry when their knees
are grazed - I said - I said - isn't that what was agreed when we were
comets, when we were fault lines, when we were tidal waves - then
she said - don't leave - she said - stay - she said - in my arms - she
said - don't leave - she said - stay.

Guernsey, Her, and Everything In Between

Perched on my chair
At the edge of a table,
Talking about

How easily glass
Shatters, even from the
Kiss of the tiniest pebble.

Opposite me
A maiden of mirrors
Amalgamates her tongue,

Bondaging me abruptly
In bandages she sews
From infantile insecurities.

She leans in,
Islands tiling her seal
(so much time spent sailing),

Clutches my collar and utters:
'Fasten your seatbelt while
Seated.'

Gleefully, I pout,
All the while intimately
Exploring her fortifications.

But all wounds heal
At some point or
Another.

Just as wood
Dampens and decays
With the passing of time.

My chair falls to pieces,
As does her grip on my neck.
This is my cue to leave.

I turn my back and crawl;
Probably best not to look
back at her sunset eyes.

Jay Farley

after Andre Bagoo
& Thom Gunn

one night

no one

& nowhere

They woke

decided to travel

westward   of West

fall   to Ocean: where it led

They would go   They traveled

emptier   of the things They knew,

ran away empty. fell   emptier, shedding

Themselves with each footprint   skin to earth

cliff face   memories   eroding   into   Sea

as They   become   less   Her   more dirt, more   Them

less

less

can you subtract   what isn't ther

Sand blows   through Them

in between the toes of Them   Sun-baked

Wind-grown   Steel skies

But if They stand   still   long enough

They take root   Dissolve

into the   Last

Mountain   so

They   keep   moving.

The path bites   time

at Their heels and Their

skin   is caked

with road still trying

to   shed

that load

Waiting on

same stale black & whites as yesterday
shades on, getting a backy to The Burlington

going back to The Burlington, shaded
hungover brash and dusk fragile

a brash hangover still dusking
watching time layered plate on plate away

wishing stale time layered plate on tectonic plate shift
work sponge down the stains of last night

sponge stains down the last night
yes I am small for the thousandth time

for the thousandth small time man again
I drag up my little black skirt for you

but my little black skirt is a drag
you cop a look at my tits my dainty legs

my dainty legs my tits exposed to you
face stuffing your full English

your full English stuffed face
pays for my minimum wage

but it's me that pays for it in the end
gender is not black & white

my gender is not this black & white
my swollen feet cry out for relief

cry out for foothold swollen relief
still waiting on living

still waiting on

Myth busters v3

What if money
was just bread and Economic Growth
was just growth. What if patriarchy
was a footnote and normal
was everyone. What if market forces
was a veg stall in St.johns. What if Eton
was an Ofsted requires-improvement-
Struggling-sports-academy-merging-with-its-neighboring-school
-so-it-didn't-close-down.
What if we were taught
how to disagree with one another. What if
divide and conquer was a kind of math
and hierarchy was a quaint parlour game. What if propaganda
clenched its fists, ground its teeth, and just
walked past. What if climate change
was a raincloud. What if altruism was impossible
because we live in a world where
all things are connected.
What if I bought
the ticket. What if I kissed you. What if your tears
weren't crocodile. What if I didn't care
what you think. What if you didn't leave me
all alone. What if you didn't
leave me alone. What if my heart wasn't
evicted. What if unconditional was
unconditional. What if
hate. What if anger. What if
war. What if greed. If
pride, if money, if bull
shit, if single-use-
lives, if
washed-up, if

selfish. What if we
were animals. What if we
were nature. What if we
were real

Jaime Starr

Beautifying the Mitzvah

1. Begin in night's rich velvet darkness. Allow loved ones snores to pass through you. Spend 60 breaths imagining their dreams. Unclench jaw. Let envy seep out.

2. Name each uncontested breath. Nourish it like a firstborn.

3. Wake. Infuse the day with longing. Whisper darkest held secret into each second until clock hands drip.

4. Find birds in late afternoon. Name them Emotion. Accept they will never be tamed, be still, never alight on your outstretched hand. Adore them anyway.

5. When hunger strikes, interrogate it. Examine which molecules crave union with you. Find them in mango and fish – use their juices to anoint the body.

6. Bless skin with sweet scent twice daily until lovers mistake you for rose, coconut, ripe pear.

7. Greet each magpie from the window, though they will not acknowledge you – invisibility is their generous gift. Return to night.

∞

Colonise OR The Bog Queen's Grave Goods

Write in a tongue not your own
Laugh with vowel sounds unfamiliar to your granny's ear
Startle her with their hostility
The lack of fáilte in your welcome
Lose your musicality
Linguistic sensuality
Replaced with triviality
Talk about the weather
Don't talk at all

Hunt in wild places
Unsubjugated bog squelches around searching fingers
Grip hard, unearth words
Buried without ceremony for their savagery
Deep in unconsecrated earth
By savage men's superiority
These neglected disinterred remnants cannot fly home
Their roost inside your mouth has long since rotted.

Lose your words
Lose your tongue
Lose your mind.

Hang a slate of shame
Around your neck
Your tongue scrubbed clean
With Queen's English
And God save if you forget it:

There's more than slates been hung for that.

∞

Nature vs Nurture

This does not come naturally
words, yes. words, natural as breathing
bleeding heart
            beat
                    one/two/three
                            words seep
                                  out
                                        with each wet thud

but this is not words
                              this *is art*

                              with capital A for Aesthetic,
                              Assonance, Alliteration,
                              Abstract, Ars Poetica.
spend evenings / pouring over dictionary

                        Before pouring becomes drowning.

diligent crafternoon / catch up
                            Catch us if you can.

Learn semicolon caresses / forward slash

                          force *their way into poetic form*

stab / wound unwelcome.

BANG HEAD AGAINST ACADEMIC CEILING
BANG HEAD AGAINST ACADEMIC CEILING
BANG HEAD AGAINST ACADEMIC CEILING

[repeat as needed]

                    until   natural   word

                                        bleeds

                                                out

Form: 1. Fabricated cuckoo egg supplants feeling.
         2. A murder, victim and villain – *acquitted with a capital A.*

                            ∞

Beth Booth

Artist Complex

There's washing on the line and the dog
sits in a sliver of sun, snout agitating
clean air and I'm afraid

of this being enough. I have some kind of
artist complex; leaves me terrified
of drinking wine in half glasses,

terrified of moving out of the city
for the quiet, of how domesticity
compromises; promised

my teenage self I wouldn't get
older, wear comfortable shoes and
a sensible haircut, give up

on beauty as though it belongs
to the young; which means
how do I love without need?

Without saving you?
How do I look at your toxic-tender face
without finding it profound?

Me: late-night wanker
discussing poetry in the pub,
interesting-like-a-car-crash

can't-look-away kind of bitch,
rash and restless and preoccupied
with truth; how do I exist

without gnawing want?
Be content without intensity?
Can I give up on

so much all the time? I want
to take a bloody bite,
to fight, to ransack life;

but there's washing on the line and the dog
sits in a sliver of sun, snout agitating
clean air and I'm afraid

of this *not* being enough. I have
some kind of artist complex;
I'm in therapy and learning

rest and rage and reliance
on more legitimate drugs. I'm learning
that we can't always keep promises

to our children, even when breaking them
is terrifying; even when our children
are ourselves.

Dovecote

1// I swear I can smell storming. Blackened skyline an inkblot above the car; my mum's hands ten-two gripping the wheel. Litany of landmarks – leylines connected by tissue of Harvester, Lidl, McDonalds, the homeless populating their steps.

2// Pigeons on the roof of the bingo gather in silent flutter, starved bodies having forgotten how we raised then abandoned them to verminhood, how they carried us homeward with messages clamped to spindle legs.

3// Pigeons leap dazzling, building falling into brick sludge and metal, and circle the car a soft grey mass. Redcurrant eyes with their sideways gape look at me and ask:

> *Do you have any idea of the magic of being one point in a cluster? Of being a perfect system?*

4// I haven't been clubbing in four years because my body is a jamming rifle, but I remember the crush of human meat: the oneness I miss like missing myself. I'm envious.

5// Pigeons look toward the sky, consumed with horizon; alight, overfilling windows and chimneys with unified hunker. My mouth is an empty chamber.

6// Look up from the street and the roofs are full of uncanny. The building yard beneath says to no one: "Be careful. Be aware. Be safe."

Museum Exhibit for the Boyfriend Who Hoped Coming Out Wouldn't Matter

first there is me crying at the party.
come here you say, overlooking that it was you
who told me your father called me weak
as though it was truth.

the plaque says:

why are you still falling in love with bi girls?
girls who've never touched each other's skin
because they're busy touching yours,
coughing down antidepressant fog
to make themselves fuckable;
why did you like me brown-haired best?
like me faking football interest?
when the cold overtook me and you maintained
that summer would return soon, why
did we both mistake that blind faith for kindness?

some people winter well, love.

but then in the display we are children
surviving the burning of our home.
it was me set the fire; fed it with kindling; blew.
chased away my own chill.

next there are the men in the pub
with loud drunk cries that might as well be weeping.
me wondering how often you weep these days;
me wondering if you still wash in those baptismal waters
without wondering who cleans the pool.

I know you try. I remember.

finally there is me, alone, waking:
one of those mornings when I have the dream
in which you skim stones across a lake
and the curvature of your spine is a coded message
on the inside of my eyelids, and
I miss you. I even miss your bullshit –
the way my skin made you nervous.

in the gift shop they sell keys.
I wonder, did you keep yours?
or maybe you locked that padlock
to a bridge years ago –
threw them into water.

Jake Evans

Dale Street 3am

Beau-ti-ful you say to me from across the road
In slow motion
Like your mouth has never tasted the word before

Your wet lips glisten in the yellow street light
Like the first piss
Hitting the toilet bowl in the morning

Glamorous girls stand knock-kneed and shivering
In silk slip dresses
Puffing hard on ciggies to keep warm

Your eyes pierce through the club lights and drunken fog
Of the night
And I - vodka brave - meet and pierce you right back

I'm floored by the dark of your stare
On the black tarmac road
And I'm lying with old gum, ciggie stubs and discarded kebabs

We undress our smiles, our clothes, our skins
And hold each other
Picked peeled naked and flesh like two ripe blood oranges

We are inside each other

We're drinking from the mouths of angels
Swimming in each other's blood
And dancing until the sun rises to burn the night to ash

In drunk-time the moment spilled out into forever
And we never really ended
In real-time we did

I forget how

Alina Burwitz

fabled

After Lucille Clifton

this body i did not choose

speak gratitudes

to red fibres - flowing over knots
like water - kissing pebbles
lengthening and shortening
all my life.

celebrate

              hollow between collarbones
              where honey pools
              like sweat, until
              the source splits and
              bluely trickles down.

                      one

        flows

left   the other

                                            right

my hills
shine with shea
freshly plucked chicken skin
wooded with little translucent hairs
rooted in puckering mounds.

from there
bubbled raised bumps spell - *kiss me* - at the centre.

from here
a down-turned mouth
disappearing into itself.

first memory of not-quite right:
my outverted little button.

little beige protrusion:
branch cut
from its mother too soon.
fingers bowed you backwards, little outtie
you
        never quite gave in to
        tiny pressing fingers.

Sing praise to pot belly:
gleefully hanging when I bend,
as it reaches for the earth.
pour red thanks from your lips,
wash pain in
hot breaths,
platitudes and
promises for
my pouch.

soak me - dip me
like stale bread -
in red
wine.

reach out
give thanks
break bread
in celebration of softness.

not quite straight

you're the little bubble in a spirit gauge
the roundness between two black lines
let me know i'm
not quite straight

O Berlin

you hung your leather shell
on the back of the door
behind my heart.

You led me with a fingertip under my chin,
let me choke on your petrol breath.

I close my eyes and see your lids,
        shining pink with sun.

O Berlin pop hubba bubba blue
in my mouth

at the Freibad.

I was your last sip
of water:
you did away with the glass,
drank me straight from the tap.

You knock back Schnapps
Rough palm curling round my nape
when we dance.
I shrug you off
/ wish I hadn't /
cos when I blink
+ rub the years from my eyes,

you've spun on.

you've begged cigs from someone else, poured liquor love into someone else's ear, pulled other seeking hands onto sticky dance floors, leaving them in the morning unfed, tangled in your bed, years falling off you, shredded silk again:

Berlin's moved on without me.

Hands between my thighs
I lie, alone,

      shut my eyes
      + see yours still open.
I peer through the spyholes in your skull
Straight into your bed.

O Berlin

      My sick little heart watches
you kick off your boots,
someone else making work
      of your idle hands,
      Undoing the belt buckle I kissed / Tugging off jeans I
watched you choose / Fucking someone I don't even know.

O Berlin.
I guzzle petrol
to taste you again.

O Berlin
I'll tell my mother
you broke my heart.

She pours honey into
broken cups:
Sticky wisdoms   i don't want
Berlin ist nix für Familien.
but mum
She is familiar
in how she holds me
Has a hold on me.

O Berlin I still feel the crook of your elbow
where I would tuck my chin
and you kissed my head

swaddled in sticky sheets.

        O Berlin you left soot
on my skin
You left dust in my lungs
I coughed out red years + sediment
that settles in bottles you drink.

                O Berlin
                My spit is cleaner now
                pink and sweeter,
                Since you left me

                but
                deep in my lungs,
                you're still there.

O Berlin I won't
        I won't
        I won't
                crawl back.

Instead
I take your shell from the door

slip myself
into your leather
       + drink in your stench.

O
Berlin

little loves

when you wash up

Your elbows dance, wide.
Send soapy tides down cracks
Neat nails curl into sponges
Jealous, I watch.
Oozing suds
Down marbled plastic, breaching
sealant, into the cupboard
Gone all swollen / deformed / won't open
              unless you yank it. Hard.
Your back sways
Want to curl
Between your shoulder blades
Break your silence.
Melamine's already peeling, MDF swelling
for you.
Winding piles of dripping dishes
I watch your hands not your face.
Did you wanna rinse that?
Sweet face all sour means, no.

I wipe, you look away.
Every. Time.

Splinters of black stubble
        on the white bathtub edge
you can't see without your glasses,
        I wipe away.

You chase dust
across the fucked kitchen lino.
Squirt kitchen spray
into   every
corner.

        Every crumb, your enemy.

I spurt
lemon yellow
down the bowl
scrub urine caked
under the seat
        orange scum out the grout,
            tired little hands.

Your tops fester
/neatly folded/
in the drawer,
wash them
all in one go,
        later.
You sigh out frustrations at
my clothes airing out
on the back of the door.
        Such a mess.

and now
it's just me

 I clean up after myself
and miss
The stains
/ The silences / the little   o   of your mouth
when your voice spills past our teeth.

And your sopping wet surfaces.
I fall into our
fingers curling into our backs
                              holding

                                        every spilling second.

pass me a tissue
pour your body
onto the mattress
next to me.

                    spill yourself, love -
                    sopping wet.
                    lumpy, grainy,
                    Like gravy from the jug:
                    sloppy -
                    And, believe me when I say
                    I'll catch every drop.

Darcy May Gillam

bedridden

ache into cotton   ceiling cracks   familiar
as veins   bucking up   on a lover's wrist
                   wrap hands   in splints   nylon tight
                   a boxer   preparing to fight   myself
a splint   is also a symptom   of an over-run horse
most common   in the young   they develop
                   beneath the knee   turn bone to knotted root
                   nerve endings to noise   bets to dust
even to the trained eye   the choreography of stress
& arousal   can be hard to tell apart
                   a gelding   having its wounded leg
                   strapped   will nod its head   the way I do
when asked   *this feel good?* the noise I make
when coming easily mistaken
                   for the stunted echo   of an injured animal
                   a stallion   hooving the track   of its mate
will flare its nostrils   the way I do   when breathing
through spasm   willing my body   to let go
                   of the crop   it uses   to beat its
            own flank
                   like a horse   pain can be ridden
to safety or into battle   unlike a horse
it can't be beaten   into submission

93

to the young

when it came to leaving

without a word or note

you unpacked yourself

& arranged your small bones

like funeral flowers

into the shape

of a sleeping

boy

breathplay

that first time
belt biting
at the fleshed
fruit of my throat
leather rooting in
merciful sickness
your familiar hand
made strange
our sex placed
in the language
of the animal
stripped
of its life's skin
thin membrane
repurposed
from its origins
to hold the body
together
at the waist
or
to carry a weapon
with the intention
of protecting life
or
taking it

Elenia Graf

Does Your Mother Know

all the greens ash   all the red tips
glowing   we not sober for a year
losing our skins   to the waves
tumbling   glorious

impersonating lobsters   learning
how to fuck   to piss in the park
and let the men watch
on our way   to DYMK

there   walls are covered in cocktail
-glass shaped mirrors   light
bouncing its blue   body
off mounted martinis

Does Your Mother Know that you
climb the metal lighting rig
every friday   friend
looking for new love

does your mother know?
yes   of the theory   but not the practice
the last time any of us were this   endless
was before our parents met

later that night   the sea licking
vodka sweat from where my breast meets my rib
us   shivering
at the bus stop before sunrise

we really walked here   children
just baptised   ready for our first
honest prayer   sweaty dykefag palms
facing the ceiling

the last time any of us were known
by   our   mothers
the glass on the walls was still
being washed   ashore

butter

i.

when i heard that my grandmother tried to kill herself with a
butter knife
i burst out laughing.

ii.

an amateur at suicide
but a pro at german dumplings.

iii.

she used to sleep in the attic
box room with a roof window
when stairs were still a possibility.
hung her coats behind the door of the bathroom
with the thimble-sized sink.

i knew she had come to visit
when the running water smelled like yves rocher.

iv.

they accused her of looking forty
to sleep with the priest.

skin so soft i kissed
molten butter from her cheek
each morning i crawled up to the attic
to watch the sun rise before school.

v.

more pearls than coins
a necklace for each colour blazer
a ruby ring she never took to lost-and-found.

vi.

when they sent her away
the red jacket on the hook bloomed.
in sleep i taste pollen
sink in the pool we visited when i was eight
wake up wondering at what age
you forget how to swim.

those mornings i prepared my breakfast rolls
and took them back to bed.
placed the plate under my pillow
like a tooth
asking the day to soften
the sheets.

vii.

she wore her bright blue suit on the ward and skipped
along the pavement when i drove to see her
so medicated she had never
had a hip replacement or
been a child
buried a child.

viii.

she sometimes told the story
of when she first felt we were one:
i was three months old and keening
at december biting my cheeks.

somehow my pain was great enough
for her to cry with me
there we were in the snow
carrying each other's weight all the way home.

ix.

two months after you die
i spread my cheeks in the mirror
to look at my arsehole
wondering who was the last
person to wipe yours clean.

x.

every time i have a spare five minutes
i itch for a transnational phone call.
please let me answer the same questions again
your words unspooled like a cassette tape.

i've quit smoking now
there's fuck all to do on my fag breaks.

xi.

the final time you breathed into a phone
it was all you could do.

xii.

i promised to catch that plane
but stayed on the ground as you left it.

xiii.

grief is your dentures in a landfill.

xiv.

ten years from now i will have decided
on the afterlife.

do you get the read the eulogies
in this language you never spoke?
calling you *grandmother*
never *oma*
calling you the only place
i wasn't afraid of the dark.

xv.

now i have your pearls
a king sized bed
sterling silver jewellery.

xvi.

do you ever lie with me those nights
when my lover is away
to wait for sunrise?

QUEER YOUR UNREST

Lightning Source UK Ltd.
Milton Keynes UK
UKHW010813091022
410080UK00004B/139